THE HAPPY FINANCES CHALLENGE

learn how to make money decisions that will lead to long-term financial happiness in just 42 days

By KARA STEVENS

Founder of The Frugal Feminista

Disclaimer:
The information contained within this book and within The Frugal Feminista website is for general information only and does not constitute professional financial advice. Please contact an independent financial professional for advice regarding your specific situation. People taking part within the challenge will have varied results. As a guide, Kara Stevens is not to be held liable for any poor results you might get from this challenge.

DEDICATION

To all women out there that KNOW that with a little help,

they could be happy, wealthy, and brave.

TABLE OF CONTENTS

INTRODUCTION

Hello Happiness Warriors!

Let me first put this out there: I love money.

Not more than I love my mom.

Not more than I love my husband.

Not more than I love my chocolate drop of a baby girl.

Not more than I love my two brothers and extended family.

Not more than I love the fierce women of The Frugal Feminista community.

No.

Saying that you love money is often perceived as being shady-cakes, greedy, slimy, sleazy, and grimy.

But it's not.

At least not for me.

One of the things that I know for sure is that people with money that are shady-cakes, greedy, slimy, sleazy, and grimy have always been that way. Money just allows them to take their shadiness to a higher level.

I love money because money is one of those things that plays such an influential role in how we see ourselves and others in the world. As a tool that creates options, it has the ability to make or break our access to success, happiness, and peace of mind in so many ways.

And you know what's crazy?

Many of us don't learn how to use it, grow it, or manage it in healthy or happy ways.

When you look around, you'll notice that many of us are walking around with limited and negative beliefs around money on one hand and conflicted feelings about it on the other.

So here's what I did.

I created The Happy Finances Challenge, (emphasis on the "happy") as a solution to all of that. When I was beginning to get my financial life in order—eliminating $65k worth of student loan debt, moving from a pauper mindset to a prosperity mindset, and building a thriving online business aka The Frugal Feminista—I had to eradicate all of the negative feelings, misinformation, mistrust, and delusions that I held about money and my worth.

With The Happy Finances Challenge, we are going to touch on the basics of money management. Equally important, but not more important, we are going to focus on what's going on in your heart, mind, and soul.

Why, you ask?

Because everything starts with thoughts, feelings, and emotions. Your decision to save vs. hoard. Your belief that you can never have what you want vs. your belief that with effort, your cash flow will grow. Your impulse to spend vs. overspend. All of these things come from a deep, deep place in your psyche.

It has been my personal experience that practical tips and tricks will take you only so far if your financial feelings are holding you and your money hostage. As my prosperity coach Joan Sotkin put it, "Financial problems are never about money and always about relationships, and financial relationships invariably have an emotional base."

Powerful, right?

So let's get to it.

Love,

WEEK 1

MONEY AND EMOTIONS

Week 1 Overview

Money and Emotions

The battle of the budget is real. It's a battle of the mind and the heart. In some peoples' heads, it may even be a war zone. When I was clawing out of $65K worth of student loan and credit card debt, I had to fight the demons that were keeping me clutching to dis-ease, distorted beliefs, and some of the ugly beliefs that I held:

Kara, you'll always be unhappy, so get used it.
See? See? Being in debt and staying in debt is inevitable.
You don't deserve to get EVERYTHING you want in life.
Being a little disappointed is a part of life.
Other people can reach their financial goals, but you can't. Your mom really hasn't.

I had to go into my financial past, unpack some of my unhealthy beliefs about money, and forgive myself for my financial mistakes in order to move on with confidence.

Why This Week Is So Important

During this week, you are going to get up close and personal with your money mindset. Since your thoughts and feelings about money inform your money decisions (thoughts → feelings → actions), we are going to spend some real time connecting with our financial identity.

Warning: You may need to purchase some tissues. I know I needed a box of Kleenex when I got financially naked and vulnerable with this week's lifework.

DAY 1

Money Memories

Today's lifework: You are going to delve into the past and get in touch with your earliest money memory.

You are going to answer: What was my earliest money memory?

- What were the smells, the people, and the sounds? What was said? What did you feel?
- Was this experience positive or negative?
- Why was this memory so vivid?
- What money message did you "learn" from this memory?

This lifework is so important because it helps you step back and see where some of your current money beliefs come from. Once you are aware of your emotions, you have so much more power to change your relationship with yourself and your money.

I'll share mine.

Kara's Earliest Money Memory

One of my earliest and most powerful money memories was when I was eight years old and my mom was paying for some sneakers for me. She looked very sad. I watched her as she looked at the register and pulled out a bill from her wallet and held it tight, like she didn't want to part with it. She held on to the money like it was the last dollar that she had.

I remember telling her, "Mom, you seem so sad when you spend money." I think that day left an indelible mark on my financial identity. I felt guilty and responsible for her budget and tried to avoid asking for things that I wanted and things that I needed.

Now, it's your turn.

My earliest money memory was…

_____
_____
_____
_____
_____
_____
_____
_____
_____
_____
_____
_____
_____
_____
_____
_____
_____
_____
_____

Share your Day 1 memory with us in The Happy Finances Community, a financial and emotional safe space on Facebook.

After you've shared in our Happy Finances Community, you can dig a little deeper. Reflect on the following question:

Do you still allow your childhood money memories to guide your adult money feelings and decisions?

DAY 2

Create a Family Tree

Today's lifework: You are going to create a family tree. But not just any family tree. A financial family tree.

Why?

You know the saying, "the apple doesn't fall from the tree"? We say that to mean that we are influenced by those around us and when we were children, we were especially influenced by our family members.

You can go to Appendix A or The Happy Finances Community (check the "files" section) and complete the "My Family Financial Tree" worksheet. You can also create a financial family tree in your journal or notebook.

When filling out "My Family Financial Tree," be sure to:

- Fill out the names of your closest family members including yourself
- Next to each person's name, jot down 2–3 messages or sayings that you've heard from them (i.e. *You only live once. I can never catch a break. Money is hard to come by.*)

There will be a second part of this lifework tomorrow for you to complete but for today, I just want you to step back and look at how your financial identity was influenced by the people around you.

What surprised you? What scared you? What empowered you?

_____

_____

_____

_____

_____

_____

_____

_____

_____

_____

_____

_____

_____

_____

_____

_____

_____

_____

_____

_____

_____

_____

_____

_____

_____

_____

_____

_____

_____

_____

_____

Take a couple of minutes to share your Day 2 "aha" moments with us in The Happy Finances Community.

DAY 3

Understanding Your Current Financial Identity

Yesterday, we went deep into your family financial tree to see who influenced your financial thinking and to see what money messages you internalized as a child.

Now you are going to focus on your financial identity.

Today's lifework: Without overthinking it, you are going to write down:

- How you feel about money
- Whose money mindset influenced you the most
- Do you want to continue to relate to money in the same way? Why or why not?

Your current financial identity...

_____
_____
_____
_____
_____
_____
_____
_____
_____
_____
_____
_____
_____
_____
_____
_____
_____
_____
_____
_____
_____
_____
_____
_____
_____
_____
_____
_____
_____

Share your Day 3 thoughts and feelings about how you are changing with respect to your money with us in The Happy Finances Community or with an accountability partner.

DAY 4

Practice Financial Forgiveness

When you know better, you do better. Period. With Days 2 and 3, you went deep and saw your financial past and present for what they really are. For some of you, this might have been really uncomfortable and unsettling.

You were probably judging yourself or even your family members for their financial missteps.

That's why today's exercise is so crucial for you to move forward.

Today's lifework: You are going to acknowledge the past but leave it behind. Let it go. It's done its part.

Here's how to let go in a few simple steps:

1. Find a quiet space in your office or home. (Lighting candles are great, but optional.)
2. You are going to sit in a comfortable position (on the floor or in a comfy chair) and you are going to envision that you are at a family dinner table.
3. At the dinner table, you are going to speak firmly and lovingly to all of the members that you listed on your family tree.
4. You are going to tell them (choose any and all that resonate with you):
   - I forgive you for not showing me…
   - I release the need to blame you for …
   - I am committed to forgiving you for…
5. After you've spoken to your family members, you are going to speak to yourself.
   - I forgive myself for…
   - I release my need to blame myself…
   - I acknowledge that I am capable of changing…

Your feelings after the forgiveness ritual...

_____
_____
_____
_____
_____
_____
_____
_____
_____
_____
_____
_____
_____
_____
_____
_____
_____
_____
_____
_____
_____
_____
_____
_____
_____
_____
_____
_____
_____

Be sure to share your Day 4 growth with us in The Happy Finances Community.

DAY 5

Write a Letter to Your Future Money

Yesterday, you freed your financial past. Even though we're influenced by those around us, it doesn't mean that we have to continue being *that* person, especially when your new/future self is waiting for you to step into your greatness.

Today's lifework: You are going to write a love letter to your money.

- Give your money a name
- Share how you want to treat her/him in the future
- Be specific about how your new financial self will manage your savings, credit cards, and debt

Today's lifework is where you really get to speak truth and abundance into your financial future. Don't be shy about how bright, happy, and at ease you want to be with your money.

As you write, you will literally be rewriting your destiny. Be deliberate with everything that you speak over and write about when it comes to your future.

Since you are charting that destiny as we speak, you want to ensure that it embodies all things that will build up your relationship with money, not break you down.

Your love letter....

_____
_____
_____
_____
_____
_____
_____
_____
_____
_____
_____
_____
_____
_____
_____
_____
_____
_____
_____
_____
_____
_____
_____
_____
_____
_____
_____
_____
_____
_____
_____
_____

Share your Day 5 love letter with us in The Happy Finances Community.

DAY 6

Create a Support System

Today's lifework: To help you connect with your new financial self, you are going to need support.

- Identify 3–5 girlfriends/family members who are ready and motivated to make changes in their financial lives. In other words, they are ready to make their finances happy.

I repeat: these girlfriends have to *already* be ready and motivated. Don't select your BFF with 17 credit cards and a weakness for late payments, red bottoms, and shunning responsibility.

Why?

You are vulnerable enough in this transition.

After you've identified your prospect for your Money Crew, you need to reach out to them.

- Text them in a group or individually: "Hey girl, I want us to support each other in getting our finances right. We can meet at my house once a week to set our financial goals. It'll be fun."
- Wait 24 hours before you follow-up with a phone call

Your thoughts…

_____
_____
_____
_____
_____
_____
_____
_____
_____
_____
_____
_____
_____
_____
_____
_____
_____
_____
_____
_____
_____
_____
_____
_____
_____
_____
_____
_____

Don't forget to share your Day 6 progress with us in The Happy Finances Community. Tell us how many accountability partners you have and when you are going to meet to talk all things money and financial freedom and happiness.

DAY 7

Week 1 Glow and Grow Report

Today is the day where you get to stop and reflect on all of your hard work and effort. Use all of the space below to consider:

- What were your biggest takeaways from this week's work?
- How are you different now than when you started on Day 1?

_____

_____

_____

_____

_____

_____

_____

_____

_____

_____

_____

_____

_____

_____

_____

_____

_____

_____

_____

_____

_____

WEEK 2

GET ORGANIZED

WEEK 2 OVERVIEW

Get Organized

During this week, we are going to organize our financial files and documents. With some basic systems and structures in place, you will feel in control and confident about your finances.

Why This Week Is So Important

Last week, we focused on mindset. We cleared the emotional clutter so you could gain a clear understanding of where you stand with your money from the inside out.

Well, this week we want your new financial "insides" to match your financial "outsides." In other words, the state of your financial environment has to reflect and match your financial internal state if you ever want to have long-term financial happiness and progress.

As with each piece of lifework, be sure to stick with it. I created lifework in bite-sized chunks so you would feel successful and accomplished every single day.

Okay, let's dig into it.

DAY 8

Create a Money Space

Today's lifework: Today, you are going to create an office. Even if it's a corner in your bedroom or on the floor. This will be your sacred money spot for you to routinely handle your finances. If you have a desk and a laptop, make sure you respect it as your money space.

In particular, for today's lifework, you will do the following:

- Clean the space thoroughly
- Beautify the space. If you have a vision board, be sure to post it near your money space. If you have flowers, place them there in a gorgeous vase.

Sidenote: Just so you know, I keep pretty pencils on my desk and a pic of Oya, a Santera goddess of destruction and change.

This step is especially important when it comes to understanding the psychology of associations. The more you associate money management with a beautiful, orderly, and peaceful space, the more positive feelings you will have with your money and your money decisions. You'll be less likely to avoid handling money or accessing your accounts because the space and vibe that you've created is so inviting and non-threatening.

What my money space shows about me....

_____

_____

_____

_____

_____

_____

_____

_____

_____

_____

_____

_____

_____

_____

_____

_____

_____

_____

_____

_____

_____

_____

_____

_____

_____

_____

_____

Post a pic of your Day 8 money space in our Happy Finances Community and let us know how you're feeling about your new money environment. It'll give all of us some inspiration.

DAY 9

Understand What Files to Keep and for How Long

Despite what you hear about financial documents, you don't have to keep all of them forever!

Today's lifework: Study the following chart so you can free yourself from believing the hype around which financial documents are necessary to keep around.

How Long to Hold Onto	Name of Document
Less Than a Year	ATM, bank deposits, and credit card receipts until you reconcile them with your monthly statements
A Year or More	Loan documents until the loan is paid off
	Vehicle titles until you sell them
	Investment purchase confirmations in stocks, bonds, mutual funds, or anything else until they are sold
Seven Years	Tax documents because the government has six years to collect the tax or start legal proceedings if you fail to report more than 25 percent of your gross income on your tax returns
Forever	Birth and death certificates, marriage licenses, divorce decrees, Social Security cards, military discharge papers, defined-benefit plan documents, estate-planning documents, life-insurance policies, and an inventory of your bank safe-deposit box (if you own one)

This chart was adapted from information from Consumer Reports. Search here for the full article on this topic. http://www.consumerreports.org/taxes/how-long-to-keep-tax-documents/

Are you thinking, *Kara, but what about those little things—daily receipts that you accumulate from living life?*

More on that on Day 10.

What financial document myth did you debunk with this chart?

_____

_____

_____

_____

_____

_____

_____

_____

_____

_____

_____

_____

_____

_____

_____

_____

_____

_____

_____

Hit us up in The Happy Finances Community and let us know what you've learned about when to "hold 'em" and "fold 'em" when it comes to your financial documents for Day 9.

DAY 10

Get to Decluttering

On Day 9, I asked you to study the rules of thumb for streamlining your financial documents. I only wanted you to analyze the chart so you could make smart decluttering decisions today.

Today's lifework: You will spend the rest of your day making five piles of documents:

- Documents that you are to keep for less than a year
- Documents that you are to keep for more than a year
- Documents that you are to keep for seven years
- Documents that you are to keep forever

I know you may be saying, "Kara, that's only four categories."

Yes, I know.

The last, and my favorite category (which, if you were like me and kept damn near every receipt since you started working) is the TRASH PILE. Yum.

If you possess documents that are too old or are not considered essential to your financial life, then you need to chuck them immediately.

Use a garbage bag and in the next section, I'll tell you how to properly dispose of these documents, especially those that have all of your personal information on them.

But for now, get to decluttering those files. Don't forget those random shoeboxes full of receipts, either!

How are you feeling about decluttering your files?

_____

_____

_____

_____

_____

_____

_____

_____

_____

_____

_____

_____

_____

_____

_____

_____

_____

_____

_____

_____

_____

_____

_____

_____

_____

_____

_____

Wooooweeee! You made it to Day 10. Share your pics, feelings, and "aha" moments in The Happy Finances Community.

DAY 11

Purchase Your Office Essentials

Yesterday, you were knee-deep in paperwork. Sorting. Shifting. Organizing. And doing so with a keen lens of what's necessary and what's not.

Great!

You should now have fewer documents in your living space. You should also feel like you have only the important documents in your money space. We needed to accomplish that so today's lifework would be useful and meaningful.

Today's lifework: Now that you know what documents you have, we are going to purchase the proper financial tools to keep them safe and organized.

- Head to your local Staples or Office Depot and purchase:
    o A scanner, a scanner app, or even your phone if you want to create e-files
    o A shredder to properly destroy documents with your personal information
    o Sufficient file folders for the four document categories
    o A safe-deposit box for papers that can't be easily replaced. Think: original birth and death certificates, Social Security cards, passports, life insurance documents, military discharge information, marriage and divorce decrees, vehicle titles, etc. This is not necessary if you are on a budget

Go to our Happy Finances Community and share your Day 11 list of office essentials.

DAY 12

Make E-files that Reflect Hard Copies

I've been told that I'm a dinosaur when it comes to all things related to books and paper. I still love my printer. Shoot me.

When it comes to maintaining and accessing documents, I think it's a good thing. (Hint: someone can steal your computer.)

But I've also seen the value in maintaining e-files as well. (Hint: There's a fire or just maybe someone steals your file cabinet.)

Today's lifework: You are going to create e-files for any of the documents that you want to have electronic access to. For me, I like to have my tax returns in digital form.

You can even consider putting them up on the cloud if that's your fancy. But be careful. Your stuff can get jacked on the cloud, too.

Here's a quick rundown of some items for which to create password-protected e-files:

- bank and investment statements
- estate-planning documents
- pension information
- insurance policies
- pay stubs
- tax documents

What files do you want to maintain as e-files?

_____

_____

_____

_____

_____

_____

_____

_____

_____

_____

_____

_____

_____

_____

_____

_____

_____

_____

_____

_____

_____

_____

_____

_____

_____

_____

_____

_____

_____

Share what you're learning from Day 12 in The Happy Finances Community.

DAY 13

Create a Financial Freedom Fund

Loose change in your purse. Loose change on your floor. Loose change in your random winter coats. Loose change under your sofa.

Sounds like a song, right? Well, maybe not!

You know that those coins add up to dollars? Hundreds and hundreds of dollars, right? But that's only if you keep them in one place. I speak from experience. I was able to use my loose change to pay for a trip to Cuba in 2008. If I'm lyin,' I'm dyin'.

Today's lifework will help you organize your itty-bitty change into big bucks.

- Get an old cookie jar, water jug, old vase, an old wastepaper basket, or a mini-trash can. It's your choice.
- Label it "My Financial Freedom Fund" (FFF)
- Decorate it and put an affirmation on it. My FFF says, "Kara, you start what you finish." You could also write a goal on it: "My Aruba trip," "My wedding gown," "My second semester book money."
- Throw all of your loose change in there at the end of each day.
  - o If you live in a house, have a few FFFs around high-traffic areas such as the kitchen and bedrooms. When necessary, combine all of the money into the central FFF.

After it has reached its capacity, redeem your coins for cash.

What will you use your FFF for? Where will you place your FFF?

_____
_____
_____
_____
_____
_____
_____
_____
_____
_____
_____
_____
_____
_____
_____
_____
_____
_____
_____
_____
_____
_____
_____
_____
_____
_____
_____
_____
_____
_____
_____

Share a pic of you and your Financial Freedom Fund in The Happy
Finances Community for Day 13.

DAY 14

Week 2 Glow and Grow Report

Today is the day where you get to stop and reflect on all of your hard work and effort. Use the space below to think about:

- What were your biggest takeaways from this week's work?
- How are you different now than when you started Week 2?
- How has your financial life changed because of Week 2?

_____
_____
_____
_____
_____
_____
_____
_____
_____
_____
_____
_____
_____
_____
_____
_____
_____
_____
_____
_____

WEEK 3

BUDGETING AND EMERGENCY FUNDS

Week 3 Overview:

Budgeting and Emergency Funds

Congratulations on making it through Weeks 1 and 2 of The Happy Finances Challenge.

You're a rock star.

During Week 3, we are going to focus on you creating a workable budget and setting realistic goals around building your emergency fund.

Why This Week Is So Important

Budgets are sexy and are easier to create than you think. More important than that, budgets are really a roadmap to how much of your income you can save, spend, and invest.

Basically, your budget is your blueprint for many of your life goals (i.e. buy a home, travel to Argentina, quit your job) and how long it will take to reach them.

Similarly, your emergency fund is created as a result of sticking to your budget and stockpiling your savings. Consider your emergency fund a life jacket for life's unexpected expenses like a car repair, a home repair, or a lost job. Even for unexpected blessings like a baby.

Real Talk

In the work that I've done with thousands of women as a coach, consultant, and speaker, I've seen that many of us don't have an income problem per se; we have a spending and budgeting problem.

This means we make more than enough money to meet all of our needs and many of our wants, but because we don't have a clear understanding of what money is coming in and out of our hands every day, week, and month, we find ourselves financially lost and depressed because we believe that we don't have enough.

By the end of this week, you and your budget will be reunited and it will feel soooo good (you know that song?). ☺

DAY 15

Crunch Your Monthly Maintenance Number

Even before we get to crunching numbers and setting budget goals, we have to stop and answer, "How much money do I *really* need to fund my life?"

Let's call it your Monthly Maintenance Number (MMN) or your cost of living.

This number is one of those crucial components of creating happy finances, but it is often overlooked.

When you know your Monthly Maintenance Number, you have more information to decide what you want to do with your time. For example, if you monthly maintenance number is very low, you can choose to quit a horrible job, decide to work part-time, take on a high-passion, low-pay project, or spend more time at home more readily than someone whose monthly maintenance number is very high.

So for **today's lifework,** I want you to go to Appendix B or The Happy Finances Community (check the "files" section) and use the Happy Finances MMN worksheet and jot down all of the spending that you do on your wants and needs throughout the month.

When you do this lifework, don't forget to:

- Be as accurate and honest as possible with your numbers (pull out your bills to help you with this super powerful process)
- Fill out the section where it says "take-home pay." We are going to need that number for tomorrow (Day 16) for creating your workable budget
- Enjoy the financial exploration and epiphanies

What is your MMN? Would you consider your MMN low or MMN high? What are you noticing and feeling about how much you are spending on your wants vs. needs?

_____

_____

_____

_____

_____

_____

_____

_____

_____

_____

_____

_____

_____

_____

_____

_____

_____

_____

_____

_____

_____

_____

_____

_____

_____

_____

Any patterns that jump out at you? Don't forget to share them in The Happy Finances Community.

DAY 16

Do the Above, Below, or Break Even Analysis

Yesterday was a powerful process for two reasons. First, it gave you insight into how much money you really need to fund your life. And second, you completed nearly 75% of what goes into creating a budget.

You wrote out all of your expenses.

The only thing left to do now is apply the *above, below,* or *break even* analysis. We need to do some simple arithmetic to help us figure that out.

For **today's lifework,** which will be two steps:

Step 1: A simple subtraction problem.

- Your monthly take-home pay *minus* your MMN (get that number from Day 15).
For example, if your take-home pay is $2,349 every month and you calculated your MMN to be $2,100 then you will be left with an extra $239 at the end of every month.
On the other hand, if your take-home pay is $2,100 every month and you calculated your MMN to be $2,349, then you will be left with a deficit of $239 at the end of every month.

  Makes sense, right?

Do your simple subtraction problem here now.

Step 2: Apply the *Above*, *Below*, or *Break Even* Analysis.

If you have a deficit of money every month, then you are… (i.e. no savings and an increase in debt)	Living Above Your Means
If you have extra money every month then you are (i.e. money to save)	Living Below Your Means
If you have a deficit of money every month then you are… (i.e. no savings, but no debt)	Living At Your Means or Breaking Even

Using the chart below, analyze what your budget is showing you about how you are living with respect to your means or money. (Above, Below, or Breaking Even).

_____

_____

_____

_____

_____

_____

_____

_____

Hold on to these numbers because we are going to need them to deepen our goal setting work around savings and building your emergency fund.

Share your Day 16 numbers in The Happy Finances Community. What did you learn from your Above, Below, Break Even analysis?

See you tomorrow! ☺

DAY 17

Choose a Budget Shortcut

Yesterday, you crunched your numbers and found out if you were living below, above, or at your means.

You might have realized that you are spending too much money on _____ (fill in the blank).

When you know what's happening on a monthly basis, you have the power to change your budget.

Here's some help for those of you who want to have a more balanced budget, one that allows you to meet all of your needs, a lot of your wants, and still *save*.

For **today's lifework**: Choose one of these guidelines if you are looking for a place to start.

Here are three different budget guidelines that will help you decide how you want to adjust your spending on wants, needs, and savings.

Rule 1: The 50:30:20 Rule is not mine though I love it. Senator Elizabeth Warren and co-author Amelia Warren Tyagi created this formula as a financial rule of thumb in *All Your Worth: The Ultimate Lifetime Money Plan*.

50 percent of your gross monthly income goes to your needs.
30 percent of your gross monthly income goes to wants.
20 percent of your gross monthly incomes goes to savings/investing.

As a rule of thumb, this can be a great place to start, but not necessarily stay when it comes to taking care of your money. You may need to adjust the ratios up or down depending on your specific financial reality at that time.

Rule 2: I came across the 70:15:15 ratio while reading *Rich Bitch: A Simple 12-Step Plan for Getting Your Financial Life* by Nicole Lapin. She uses the **3E** rule for budgeting.

70 percent of your gross monthly income goes toward **essentials** (housing, food, transportation)

15 percent of your gross monthly income goes toward your **endgame** (retirement, savings)

15 percent of your gross monthly income goes toward your **entertainment or extras**. With this strategy, make sure that you pay for all of your entertainment in cold, hard cash so you can avoid racking up tacky credit card debt. (Yeah, I called unnecessary consumer debt "tacky"... because it is a sight for sore eyes.)

Rule 3: Here are general guidelines for a healthy budget endorsed by many in the personal finance niche.

Housing 35%: This includes mortgage, rent, taxes, repairs, improvements, or renovations, insurance, utilities, and any other expenses pertaining to the maintenance and upkeep of the home.

Transportation 20%: This category includes monthly car payments, gas, oil, repairs, insurance, parking, and public transportation fees.

Debt 15%: Basically any debt except your mortgage and car payment should be placed into this category including credit cards, personal loans, or student loans.

Personal Expenses 20%: Here you have all additional "cost of living" expenses such as food, insurance, prescriptions, clothing, entertainment, dental, medical, prescriptions, or any other miscellaneous expenditures.

Investments & Savings 10%: This category includes stocks, bonds, savings, retirement plans, rental properties, or artwork.

The Rule of Thumb for Rules of Thumb

Now for some real talk about rules of thumb. They are just that: shortcuts that can work in a lot of cases, but not in all. If you know that your goal is to eliminate debt, then you can increase the percentage that you put towards your endgame by 20, 30, 40 percent or more.

If you know yourself to be a bit of a miser and see parts of your life that would benefit from consistently spending money on personal or career development, then you may have to loosen up your saving percentage goals.

Share in our Happy Finances Community which rule of thumb works for you and why.

DAY 18

Pick an Emergency Fund Goal with My 6:9:12 Rule

As you know, an emergency fund is the money you squirrel away to keep you from making a financial inconvenience a financial catastrophe.

While a job loss is unfortunate, it doesn't have to bury you financially if you've socked away enough to weather this financial storm.

You know what they say, "You never have to get ready if you are always ready."

The best way to stay ready is to build a sexy, rainy day–proof emergency fund. Here's my 6:9:12 Emergency Money Rule to help you stay focused and targeted.

Six months of living expenses or net income:[*] If you are living in an expensive city, this is a bare minimum to hold you over in the event of a job loss, a medical expense, or any other unforeseen emergency. Keeping this amount of money will keep you from relying on credit cards, which could transform a financial emergency

---

[*] Living expenses include the total amount of money you spend to cover basics like food, clothing, transportation, entertainment, and rent/mortgage every month. In theory, your living expenses should not exceed your net income, which is amount of money you bring home after taxes each pay period. Living expenses can vary while net income is usually a fixed amount every month.

In my experience, aiming to build an emergency fund based on net income is the more ambitious goal since your net income should exceed your living expenses on a monthly basis. Similarly, your living expenses can fluctuate depending on how well you reduce costs every month.

into a financial disaster. In other words, this emergency fund saves you from going into debt.

Nine to twelve months of living expenses or net income: It would be wise to save this amount of cushion if you are self-employed, your income fluctuates (i.e. if you rely heavily on commissioned-based transactions), or if you work in a declining industry with lots of layoffs.

Twelve months of living expenses or net income: Save this amount of money if you earn $100,000 or more. There are fewer jobs offering this salary, so your job hunt may be longer than the typical candidate that is seeking positions for more modest salaries.

You also want to save this amount if your job is highly specialized as it may take more time to find a job in your field. Independent of job replacement, it would be ideal for you to save this amount in your emergency fund if you have dependents and children.

Now that you know my 6:9:12 rule on emergency funds, you're going to choose one for today's **lifework.** Write down why this emergency fund goal works for you.

_____
_____
_____
_____
_____
_____
_____
_____
_____
_____
_____
_____
_____
_____

_____
_____
_____
_____
_____
_____
_____
_____
_____
_____
_____
_____
_____
_____
_____
_____
_____
_____
_____
_____
_____
_____
_____
_____
_____
_____
_____
_____
_____
_____
_____
_____
_____
_____

Also, please share your choice in the Happy Finances Community.

DAY 19

Create an Action Plan to Build Your Savings and
Emergency Fund Goals (Part I)

Since your budget is personal and customized to where you are in life
right now, it's hard to say what a good budget is versus a bad budget.
The only hard line that I can draw is that if you're living above your
means or at your means, then it's in your best financial interest to
find ways to:

1) decrease your spending
2) increase your income
3) do both
4) do both on steroids

Today, we are only going to focus on Strategy #1.

For today's lifework: Look at your budget and see where you could
decrease your spending.

Now that you see where you could decrease your spending, it's now
time to create an action plan about *how*. Brainstorm your ideas below.

_____
_____
_____
_____
_____
_____
_____
_____
_____
_____

_____

_____

_____

_____

_____

_____

_____

_____

_____

_____

_____

_____

_____

_____

_____

_____

_____

_____

_____

_____

_____

_____

_____

_____

_____

_____

_____

_____

_____

_____

_____

Share how you can decrease your spending in your budget for Day 19 in The Happy Finances Community.

DAY 20

Create an Action Plan to Build Your Savings and
Emergency Fund Goals (Part II)

I thought you would need an additional day to continue building your
action plan to stockpile your savings and emergency funds.
Yesterday, you focused on the many ways that you would decrease
your spending.

For today's lifework, I want you to focus on Strategy #2. What are
the many ways that you could increase your income? If you need
some ideas, check out 100 Easy Side Hustles in Appendix C for some
ideas.

_____

_____

_____

_____

_____

_____

_____

_____

_____

_____

_____

_____

_____

_____

_____

_____

_____

_____

_____
_____
_____
_____
_____
_____
_____
_____
_____
_____
_____
_____
_____
_____
_____
_____
_____
_____
_____
_____
_____
_____
_____
_____
_____
_____
_____
_____
_____

Share your income-generating strategies in The Happy Finances Community.

DAY 21

Automate Your Savings Goals

Today is a fun day. You get to put your savings on auto-pilot in a few ways and watch your coins grow!

So for **today's lifework**, try out any of these hacks to automate your savings and emergency fund goals.

Set up automated deductions to your savings account. You can do this in a few easy-peasy steps.

First, make sure you have a savings account and that it's linked to your checking account.

Second, if you have direct deposit (if not, seriously consider it), have your savings goal automatically deposited into your savings account. Remember if your goal is to save $1,000 per month and you get paid twice a month, you're going to schedule a $500 deduction from each check.

If you don't have direct deposit, there is still an easy option available: set up an automatic transfer from your checking account to your savings account every time you're paid. For example, if you're paid every other Friday, establish an automatic transfer of a set amount of money from checking to savings to coincide with this deposit.

Just make sure you're aware of when the money will be deducted each month, or you may find yourself overdrawn.

Use responsive apps like Digit and Level Money: To use Digit, you need to connect your checking account. This allows Digit to analyze your income and spending, and find small amounts of money it can safely set aside for you. Every two or three days, Digit transfers some money (usually $5–$50) from your checking account to your Digit savings.

Similarly, when you use Level Money, it allows you to plan for necessary expenses and to set a savings goal. It informs you of the leftover money you have, dubbed as "spendable" money. The app informs you how much spendable money you have spent each month, and how much you have left to spend with a simple graphic. What's also very cool and helpful is that it tracks and groups expenses month-to-month or annually. Plus, it features a daily spending guide to help you stay on track.

Let us all know in The Happy Finances Community how you're going to automate your emergency fund and savings goals.

DAY 22

Week 3 Glow and Grow Report

Today is the day where you get to stop and reflect on all of your hard work and effort. Use the space below to think about:

- What were your biggest takeaways from this week's work?
- How are you different now than when you started Week 3 on Day 15?
- How has your financial life changed because of Week 3?

_____
_____
_____
_____
_____
_____
_____
_____
_____
_____
_____
_____
_____
_____
_____
_____
_____
_____
_____

WEEK 4

DITCH YOUR DEBT

Week 4 Overview

Ditch Your Debt

Congratulations on making it through Weeks 1, 2, and 3 of The Happy Finances Challenge.

You are really in it to win it.

During Week 4, we are going to focus on helping you get on top of your debt and create a plan that will help you demolish your debt in a way that works for your budget and your goals.

In other words, we are going to create a debt elimination plan that does NOT make you feel deprived, dry, ashy, and all conflicted about paying off your debt.

We will not use a deprivation model to help you eliminate your debt.

Why This Week Is So Important

One of the easiest ways to build AND maintain wealth is to get rid of your debt and keep a debt-free lifestyle.

From the thousands of women that I have worked with and from personal experience, how you relate to money changes when you see your way out of debt.

You make it your business not to get back in it. You make it a priority to safeguard your wealth from frivolous expenses. You learn how to take care of your needs and most of your wants.

It's one of the most spiritual experiences that you could go through with your money. Without debt, you get to see what life has to offer, you have the opportunity to live aligned with your purpose, and you feel a sense of connection and hope that makes life that much more full and fulfilling.

Real Talk: What You Should Remember

Most of your friends and family are in debt, so your goal of eliminating debt may not seem that important to them. Heck, most Americans live knee-deep in debt and while they (in theory) want to get out it, debt has become a natural part of their lives like breathing.

So don't expect a cheerleading squad. You may even see a few green-eyed bandits surface when they see your financial progress and ultimate freedom. That's why I told you to build a support network back on Day 6.

DAY 23

Get Your Credit Card Debt Stats

To get rid of your debt, you must start from the beginning. I can't tell you how many women I've worked with either underestimate or overestimate how much debt they have.

In the case of underestimating, they walk around with a false sense of financial security which leads them to make financial decisions that do not benefit them in the long run because they think they are more fluid than they really are.

On the flip side, I've worked with women that have overestimated the amount of their debt. In these cases, they harass themselves with unnecessary feelings of shame and regret around their finances when a quick stat check would have provided them with an accurate starting point for their debt elimination plan of action.

So **today's lifework:**
- o Please jot down all of your credit card debt to the penny. Please include debt accumulated on all of your credit cards and store cards. Open the bills, check online, or call your lender to ensure that the numbers are accurate.
- o Please write down the interest rates attached to each of the cards.
- o Calculate the total amount of outstanding credit card debt you have.

You can jot this down in your journal, below in the spaces that I provide you, or go to The Happy Finances Community and download your Get Your Credit Card Debt Stats or CCD Stats worksheet.

You can also find this worksheet in Appendix D.

Today, just take a look at where you stand with your debt.

Write down all of your debt below.

Name of Credit Card/Store Card	Outstanding Balance	Interest Rates
	Total Debt:	

What have you noticed about your total amount of debt? Have you overestimated or underestimated the amount? How are you feeling?

_____

_____

_____

_____

_____

_____

_____

_____

_____

Please let us know about this process in The Happy Finances Community. How did it feel to write down your debt? What thoughts came to mind? What feelings and sensations did you have?

DAY 24

Create a SMART Goal for Your Debt

So yesterday, you probably had a come-to-Jesus moment when you saw all of your debt in black and white.

But let me tell you, with time, you will be free of it.

I promise.

And that's what today's lifework is about.

For **today's lifework**: you will create a SMART goal for your debt. I LOVE SMART goals. SMART is an acronym for Specific, Measurable, Accurate, Realistic, and Time-bound.

And SMART goals are perfect for debt goals because it breaks your big goals of being debt free into yearly, monthly, and even daily goals.

So instead of saying something vague like, "I want to get rid of all of my debt," you create a SMART goal like this, "I want to eliminate $30,000 worth of debt in five years. That means I will eliminate $6,000 in each of those five years. On a monthly basis, I will need to eliminate $500 of debt. On a weekly basis, I will need to find an extra $125 a week to reach this goal."

Now let's do the SMART analysis of this debt goal.

Was it specific? Absolutely! $30K in five years → $6k per year → $500 per month → $125 per week.

Was it measurable? Absolutely! When you work in dates, numbers, and time, by nature it's measurable.

Was it accurate? Well, using Day 22 stats should make it accurate.

Was it realistic? We are going to say yes. We don't believe in self-sabotage so we don't create unicorn-like goals.

Was it time-bound? Yes. In five years from now, the debt should be dead.

I'll say it again.

How much time do you realistically think it will take to pay off your debt in a way that doesn't make you feel dry, deprived, longing, and wanting?

I say this because too many of us create big lofty goals of paying five-figure debt with a four-figure income in less than two years.

I know I had that feeling when I took out my second set of loans for graduate school and realized that I had to repay $40K. (Dear Lord!)

That's a recipe for disaster.

I don't want to set you up for failure. Only success when it comes.

Okay, I've talked enough.

Time for **lifework.**

It's your turn to get SMART with your debt. Don't be a hero or a superwoman when creating your SMART goal(s). You want to create a goal that works for you and no one else but you. No one is watching except you.

_____
_____
_____
_____
_____
_____
_____
_____
_____
_____
_____
_____
_____
_____
_____
_____
_____
_____
_____
_____
_____
_____
_____
_____
_____
_____
_____
_____

And don't forget to share your SMART goals in The Happy Finances Community.

DAY 25

Know Your *How*

Now that you have a SMART goal (aka time table) for eliminating your debt, now we are going to figure out the best way for **you** to do so.

I emphasize *you* because no one lives your life and no one knows the intimacies of your financial life better than you do.

When it comes to eliminating debt, there is no right or wrong way to eliminate it. The only way that you get the debt elimination game wrong is when you decide to do nothing and keep your head in the sand.

So for **today's lifework**, you are going to review two strategies for eliminating debt and you are going to choose ONE.

Option #1: High-interest balance method: With this method, you organize your outstanding debt in order from highest to lowest interest rate. The rationale for this method is reasonable.

There are financial pundits that want you to save as much money as possible by eliminating the debt with the highest interest rate first. And technically, they are right.

When you have any outstanding balance (i.e. $300) with a high-interest rate (25%), it is costing you more to keep that balance "alive" than an outstanding balance with the same balance but with a lower, different interest rate (10%).

But as we know money ain't rationale. Hence, option #2, which is the one that I used during my debt elimination journey.

Option #2: Smallest balance method: With this method, you list your debt balances in order from smallest to largest without paying attention to interest rates. If, however, you have two bills with the same balance but different interest rates, you can decide how you want to list them. For example, if Credit Card A has a balance of $1,000 with a 20% interest rate and Credit Card B has a balance of $1,000 with a 15% interest rate, it'll be up to you to decide how you'll want to list these two debts. No way is better than the other; just make a decision and move on with the process. With this method, you get an immediate, quick win, which is so important for staying motivated.

So for today's **lifework,** you are going to choose a method and commit to it.

Circle your option below:

High-interest Rate Method OR Small Balance Method

Why did you choose this method? What about this method resonates with your personality and your financial goals?

_____

_____

_____

_____

_____

_____

_____

_____

_____

_____

_____

_____

_____

_____

_____

_____

_____

For Day 25, share which option you'll use in The Happy Finances Community and why that's your choice.

DAY 26

Organize Your Debt Based on Your *How*

Today's **lifework** will help you get down to the nitty-gritty. Take the debt list that you made on Day 22 and organize it based on the big debt decision that you made yesterday.

If you chose the small balance method, then organize your debt from the smallest to the largest amount and ignore the amount of interest.

If you chose the high-interest method, then organize your debt from Day 22, placing the bill with the highest interest rate at the top.

This lifework alone will make you feel *so* in control of your financial present and financial future.

Now that you know what your debt is and how you will tackle it, I know you are probably thinking: *Kara, how in the heck am I going to actually find the money to get this debt out of my life?* And I bet you are probably also asking, "How long will it take me to get rid of this damn debt?"

Take a breath. You have done so much good lifework already.

And remember I got you. We'll have answers to both of these questions over the next few days.

What are you learning about your approach to debt elimination from Day 26? Share them with me and the rest of The Happy Finances Community.

DAY 27

Know Your Rights

For most of this week, I assumed that you were dealing with debt that has NOT gone into collections.

But I know some of you have debt that has gone into collections and you have a lot questions about how to stop the debt collectors from calling, how to negotiate your outstanding debt, and a lot more questions that pertain to your specific financial situation.

Today's **lifework** is about building your knowledge and getting more support.

Under the Fair Debt Collection Practices Act, federal law sets down a specific set of rules that third-party debt collectors must follow when contacting you about a debt. Debts covered under this law include auto loans, medical bills, and credit card bills.

They **can't** do some of the following unfair and deceptive practices to collect debt from you:

- Call you at all types of hours. They can only call between 8 a.m. and 9 p.m., and not at times deemed inconvenient to you, the consumer, unless you have given them permission to call you at other times.
- Call repeatedly in a short period of time in order to harass you.
- Threaten that you will go to jail or that they will make the debts public.
- Call your employer about your debt, unless it represents unpaid child support.

- Call you again if you tell them not to do so, but their collection efforts can continue.
- Garnish your wages or take other personal property to satisfy the debt. In order for that to happen, they must sue you in a court of law and obtain a court judgment. The federal government is one of the only creditors allowed to garnish without such a judgment.
- Cash post-dated checks early.
- Charge you any fees, penalties, or interest that was not agreed to in the original contract with the creditor.

Bookmark these sites

You may report any trouble you may have with a creditor or collection agency to your state's Attorney General's office (http://www.naag.org/) and the Federal Trade Commission (http://www.ftc.gov/).

You can also review the terms of the Fair Debt Collection Practices Act on the Federal Trade Commission's website: http://www.ftc.gov/bcp/edu/pubs/consumer/credit/cre18.shtm.

Share something new you learned about your rights from Day 27 in The Happy Finances Community.

DAY 28

Get More Support

Get free bona fide support from credit counselors for no charge. There are a lot of shady, dodgy establishments that will try to charge you to help you get out of debt (the irony). To be on the safe side, head over to The United States Department of Justice for a list of approved credit counseling agencies by state and judicial district.

It will be hard work and you may not like what they have to say, but if you commit to change and do what you are supposed to do, you will be able to make deep dents in your debt, which will make your credit jump, your bank account grow, and your peace of mind expand.

And ain't nothing sweeter than that.

Now, today's **lifework**:

- Look at The United States Department of Justice site, select your state, U.S. territory, or commonwealth from the dropdown list
- Identify two or three agencies that best fit your credit and debt elimination goals
- Take a look at what they have to offer and schedule an appointment if you need to

For Day 28, share with us what you learned about these organizations in The Happy Finances Community.

DAY 29

Week 4 Glow and Grow Report

What are your financial reflections for this week? How will you tackle your debt? What are your new learnings?

_____
_____
_____
_____
_____
_____
_____
_____
_____
_____
_____
_____
_____
_____
_____
_____
_____
_____
_____
_____
_____
_____
_____
_____

WEEK 5

BE YOUR OWN BOSS

WEEK 5 OVERVIEW

Be Your Own Boss

Throughout this challenge, we focused on how to manage the money that you already have before we even touched on the concept of being your own boss through entrepreneurship or side-hustlin'.

This was on purpose.

Why This Week Is So Important

If I started this challenge teaching you that the best way to happy finances is through making more money and you still didn't have a budget, didn't have a debt elimination plan, and didn't heal your relationship with money, how do you think you would treat any new money that came into your life?

Exactly.

You would still have the same problems but instead of dealing with smaller amounts of money problems, you would be dealing with larger amounts of money problems.

Imagine a house without a sturdy foundation and you decide to add another floor to the house. Disaster. The house will cave in.

But now that you have a strong foundation on how to manage what you have, we can start thinking strategically about how to make you more.

Yum! Enjoy this week.

Even though the process of starting your side hustle is a very involved process and there are tons of books (with lots of pages) about the topic, I'm going to help you begin the process of thinking like an entrepreneur!

DAY 30

Find Your Sweet Spot

The first step in becoming your own boss is to figure out what goods or services you want to sell.

You start by finding what I call your "sweet spot."

Your sweet spot is the place where what you love to do (and do well) meets what people are willing to pay for.

What you love + what you do well + able to monetize = sweet spot.

Remember this formula as you do your lifework today. Because you need to have *all three elements* to find your sweet spot.

For example, I love to nap. But since no one is going to pay me for that, then it's not my sweet spot. While I love to sing, I've been told on several occasions that I could not carry a note to save my life. So a solo career headlining for Bey is probably not in the stars.

But…

I love writing, teaching, speaking, and coaching about all things finance and feminism, and I've been paid by companies and individuals to help them elevate their financial acumen and their understandings of feminism. In essence, I found my sweet spot.

So for **today's lifework,** you are going to get a good idea of what your sweet spot is.

Here are two options to help you find your sweet spot.

Option #1: Use the formula.
What you love + what you do well + able to monetize = sweet spot.

When you use this option, ask yourself some of the following questions:

- o Can I see myself doing this for a few years?
- o How do I know that I do it well? What evidence do I have?
- o Have other people been paid to do the same thing?

Option #2: Text, email, or call ten people in your network and tell them that you want to start a side business and tell them you need their input in finding your sweet spot.

Do your dreaming and planning below:

_____
_____
_____
_____
_____
_____
_____
_____
_____
_____
_____
_____
_____
_____
_____
_____
_____

_____
_____
_____
_____
_____
_____
_____
_____
_____
_____
_____
_____
_____
_____
_____
_____
_____
_____
_____
_____
_____
_____
_____
_____
_____
_____
_____
_____
_____
_____
_____
_____

Tell us about your sweet spot in our Happy Finances Community.

DAY 31

Figure Out How You Want to Sell Your Sweet Spot

On Day 30, you found your sweet spot—something that you love doing, are good at, and people are willing to pay for.

Let me tell you, that's probably the most difficult task to do, especially if you have a lot of passions and are awesome at all of them.

You can really insert your jazz hands here.

Today's lifework is taking that sweet spot and deciding how you will make money from it. In the world of sales, you are either the owner of a product, a service, or both.

To get your juices flowing, here are a few ways that you can take your passion and make it a service or product.

- o Speak as a keynote speaker or workshop leader on your topic of passion
- o Train individuals and organizations to make them an expert on your topic of passion
- o Consult with individuals and organizations with advice, feedback, and resources on how to make what they do better based on your expertise
- o Freelance with companies and individuals by offering your area of expertise for a fee
- o Coach individuals and groups on how to remove obstacles (perceived or real) so they can reach your level of expertise with respect to your passion
- o Host your own live events, conferences, and retreats where you go into detail about your topic from various perspectives

or bring in other experts to do so. They can range in length from three hours to several days.

o Make digital products like worksheets, ebooks, and audiobooks

o Make physical products like journals, t-shirts, workbooks, paperback books, mugs, hair products, skin products, and jewelry

o Blog and vlog to share your passion about your topic for free so you can offer products and services to die-hard fans at a fee down the line. It also allows you to sell other people's products and services that you trust for an affiliate commission.

o Lead your online classes, courses and programs through webinars, teleseminars, online home study courses, and audio/video programs

Now it's your turn. Brainstorm below *how* you want to sell your sweet spot. Remember, you can always come back and change it, but the most important thing is that you start NOW.

_____

_____

_____

_____

_____

_____

_____

_____

_____

_____

_____

_____

_____

_____

_____

_____

Now we need you to spread the love. Make sure you share your Day 31 revelations in The Happy Finances Community.

DAY 32

Create a Schedule to Work on Your Side Hustle

Now that you've narrowed down what you love to do (and do well) and decided how you wanted to make money from it, it's time to create a schedule so you can begin to take your side hustle from an idea to an income creator.

Usually, if you are just starting out and working your full-time job, you have only a few options for side-hustling.

They include working during the following times:

- o Mornings (before work)
- o Evenings (after work)
- o Lunchtime
- o Weekends
- o Sick time
- o Vacation time

When I decided that I wanted to start The Frugal Feminista, my freelance writing, and my other projects around healing and helping women with their personal growth and personal finances, I committed at least 10 hours a week to this work.

So for **today's lifework,** you are going to make a schedule for when you will work your business.

Do so below:

_____

_____

_____

_____

_____

_____

_____

_____

_____

_____

_____

_____

_____

_____

_____

_____

_____

_____

_____

_____

_____

_____

_____

_____

_____

_____

_____

_____

_____

Go to The Happy Finances Community and let us know what your side hustle schedule is for Day 32.

DAY 33

Immerse Yourself in Your Passion (aka Find Your Crew)

As you get into your passion-based side hustle, a lot of questions are going to surface: How should I price my products? What should I blog about? What topics should go into my workshops? What's a media kit? How do I create a tutorial?

As a newbie, you have the benefit of being surrounded by people (online and offline) doing what you want to do. It's just a matter of how you want to find your crew.

So for **today's lifework,** I want you to consider how you will build relationships with people in your industry as you begin to grow your side hustle.

Here are a few ways to begin the process:

- o Identify 10–15 people in the industry that you want to break into and ~~stalk~~ study everything that they do. Go to their sites, buy their products, sign-up for their mailing lists so you can really get a deep understanding of what they offer, how they offer it, and more importantly, how *you* are different from them
- o Join Facebook groups based on your interest
- o Offer to interview them for your site or publication
- o Comment on their work publicly via your social media outlets
- o Email the experts that you want to emulate. Be sure that you are not looking to "pick their brain." Be a big girl and invest in their services to show goodwill and that you are interested in a mutually-beneficial relationship

Now it's your turn. How will you begin to connect with those in your community? What other ways can you think of to make connections?

_____
_____
_____
_____
_____
_____
_____
_____
_____
_____
_____
_____
_____
_____
_____
_____
_____
_____
_____
_____
_____
_____
_____
_____
_____
_____
_____
_____

Since we are your crew, share how you'll use The Happy Finances Community to help you achieve your goals for Day 33.

DAY 34

Create a Budget for Your Side Hustle

Recently in one of my Facebook groups, I read a post from a woman who cursed the day that she left her full-time job to start her business because she ran out of money only after two months.

It's clear that she didn't want to use the money from her full-time job to build her side hustle until it became a full-fledged business, but this really is an excellent practice since making the first dollars from your side hustle could take weeks or months.

So for **today's lifework,** I need you to start thinking about how much of your full-time income you'll invest in your side hustle—will you invest a percentage of your income (i.e. 5%? 10%?) or will it be a specific dollar amount?

This is really important for two reasons. It helps you make daily money decisions from the perspective of a business owner instead of a consumer. The $20 that you blow on drinks every Friday can now be $20 that you invest into a virtual assistant. See the difference?

So looking back at your budget from Week 3, how will you make room in your budget for your business? Remember, this is an investment with long-term returns.

How much will you put aside for your business each month? What will you use that money for? Plan below for the first six months.

_____

_____

_____

_____

_____

_____

_____

_____

_____

_____

_____

_____

_____

_____

_____

_____

_____

_____

_____

_____

_____

_____

_____

_____

_____

_____

_____

_____

_____

Share your Day 34 side-hustle budget with us in The Happy Finances Community.

DAY 35

Put Yourself Out There

This is a scary but necessary part of doing a side hustle. It is time to let your light shine. Tell everyone that you know that you are open for business.

Here are a few low-cost ways to get started:
- o Announce it on your favorite social media sites
- o Send an email blast to your friends and family
- o Host an intimate event announcing your business intentions and ask for referrals
- o Create business cards and target 5–10 places and/or individuals that you would like to work with

Now, It's your turn. For today's **lifework**, think about how you will let everyone know you're open for business.

_____
_____
_____
_____
_____
_____
_____
_____
_____
_____
_____

_____
_____
_____
_____
_____
_____
_____
_____
_____
_____
_____
_____
_____
_____
_____
_____
_____
_____
_____
_____
_____
_____
_____
_____
_____
_____
_____
_____
_____
_____

Spill the beans on how you'll put yourself out there.

DAY 36

Week 5 Glow and Grow Report

How have you grown in understanding yourself as an entrepreneur during this week? What have you learned?

_____

_____

_____

_____

_____

_____

_____

_____

_____

_____

_____

_____

_____

_____

_____

_____

_____

_____

_____

_____

_____

_____

_____

_____

_____

WEEK 6

FINANCIAL SELF-CARE
ROUTINES & BOUNDARIES

Week 6 Overview

Financial Self-Care Routines & Boundaries

Woohoo! You've made it to the final week of The Happy Finances Challenge.

By now you've learned so much about budgeting, debt elimination, organizing your files, improving your money mindset, and growing your money through entrepreneurship.

So in this final week, we are going to shore up your financial self-care routines and boundaries.

Say what?

What I mean is that this week, we are going to ensure that you learn how to continually treat yourself in a loving and accepting way when it comes to dealing with your money and when dealing with your friends and family members.

Why This Week Is So Important

As you grow in your finances, you will encounter friends and family members that will not be as invested in their financial growth and will expect you to be their ATM, their co-signer, and their personal venture capitalist.

You will have to learn how to be strong and steady so their financial problems don't become *your* financial problems.

Also, you will inevitably have trips, slips, and dips when you are making changes in your financial world. And I want to make sure you have all of the support to rebound with a quickness.

DAY 37

Learn to Say "No" to Financial Requests

One of the unspoken reasons that many women can't save is because they have unofficially been identified as the family ATM.

Now there is nothing wrong with being generous when you can. But all too often, women are giving money that they can't afford and are suffering in silence about it.

No more.

So for **today's lifework,** we are going to give you a few strategies on ways to protect your pockets as well your emotions.

Strategy #1: Just say "no"

This is probably the most straightforward way of dealing with the issues. But for ladies new to financial self-care, it can also be the hardest. If you have the moxie to do so and stand firm in your no, then use this strategy often.

Strategy #2: Have a prepared phrase that is at once vague and specific enough to let them know that you ain't gonna come up off your cash

Here is my favorite: "Sorry, my finances aren't allowing me to do that right now." And if you can push yourself to get comfortable with an awkward silence, you will be empowered to use this structure in other areas of your life.

Strategy #3: Craft a firm email

If you are not light on your feet when it comes to having conversations about money, use technology as a buffer. Get your thoughts together about what you want to say. If you need to save it in a draft in order to revise and edit over the course of a few days, then do so.

Once you feel that you have conveyed your feelings, expectations, and limits, press send. The beauty of technology is that even with an immediate reply from the recipient, you can respond at your own pace.

Strategy #4: Play defense

If you agree to lend money, don't be so fast to dish out the money without a paper trail. You are well within your right to draw up a contract that specifies how much was borrowed, when it will be repaid, and the consequences for failure of repayment. Sometimes this conversation alone will make them back down from the ask. Giving details about how you will be repaid will be too much of a hassle. (Go figure).

So which of these strategies resonate the most with you? Why? What else could you say or do to say "no" to financial requests?

_____
_____
_____
_____
_____
_____
_____
_____
_____
_____
_____
_____
_____
_____
_____
_____
_____
_____
_____
_____
_____
_____
_____
_____
_____
_____
_____
_____
_____
_____

How will you say "no"? Share your favorite strategy in The Happy Finances Community.

DAY 38

Create a Go-to List of Frugal Luxuries

It's important that you stop and celebrate the progress that you make along your financial journey.

The key to celebrating your success is finding low-cost, high-value activities and items that will bring you joy and not break your bank.

I know for me, buying a good book and treating myself to a latte and a chocolate chip cookie are ways that I love to celebrate a major breakthrough. Case in point—after writing this section, I'm going to a local café for a mocha latte.

So for **today's lifework,** you are going to make a list of at least 15 activities or items that bring you joy but won't break your bank. Try to keep the items to $25 (tax included) or less.

_____
_____
_____
_____
_____
_____
_____
_____
_____
_____
_____
_____
_____

_____

_____

_____

_____

_____

_____

_____

_____

_____

_____

_____

_____

_____

_____

_____

_____

_____

_____

_____

_____

_____

_____

_____

_____

_____

_____

_____

_____

_____

_____

Share the highlights of your frugal luxuries list in The Happy Finances Community for Day 38.

DAY 39

Consider Volunteering Your Time & Donating Your Money to Causes You Believe In

Philanthropy is an awesome way to practice financial self-care. With even $5, you can contribute to a larger cause and know that your money really has meaning and power and the ability to change the world.

If you've never thought about donating to a cause, let that be the focus of **today's lifework.**

Research between five to ten organizations whose mission aligns with your values and donate what you are able to. If you can't think of any, use a site like www.charitynavigator.org to give you some guidance.

_____
_____
_____
_____
_____
_____
_____
_____
_____
_____
_____
_____
_____
_____
_____

_____

_____

_____

_____

_____

_____

_____

_____

_____

_____

_____

_____

_____

_____

_____

_____

_____

_____

_____

_____

_____

_____

_____

_____

_____

If you can't donate money, that's okay. You can donate time or even use your social media networks to share their mission with your friends and family.

What organizations made your short list? Share the outcomes of your research for Day 39 in The Happy Finances Community.

DAY 40

Conduct a Time Audit

It's almost noble in our society (especially if you are a woman) to run around like a chicken with its head cut off. Being busy, frazzled, and out of breath almost seems to be the norm.

The health and financial consequences of being so busy are real. You get sick, you rush and hurt yourself, or you become forgetful and have to buy things two and three times over.

And the list can go on and on.

For **today's lifework**, you are going to think very deeply about how you use all of your time on a daily basis and if you actually enjoy what you are doing that day.

From the time that you wake up until the time that you go to bed, what exactly are you doing with your time? Consider this process a form of deep-diving and self-analysis.

Morning
From 6 a.m. to noon, what did I do and how did I feel about it?

Afternoon
From 12 p.m. to 5 p.m., what did I do and how did I feel about it?

Evening
From 5 p.m. to 9 p.m., what did I do and how did I feel about it?

Late Night
From 9 p.m. to bedtime, what did I do and how did I feel about it?

_____
_____
_____
_____
_____
_____
_____
_____
_____
_____
_____
_____
_____
_____
_____
_____
_____
_____
_____
_____
_____
_____
_____
_____
_____
_____
_____
_____
_____

What has your Day 40 time audit revealed to you? Share your thoughts in The Happy Finances Community.

DAY 41

Get More Help (If You Need It)

If you've followed my freelance writing and topics of interest on The Frugal Feminista, you know that I'm an adamant advocate of therapy. Growing up, I was exposed to a lot of family chaos and some of the ways that I coped with the pain was through unhealthy spending and eating habits.

Sound familiar?

If you think you need to talk to someone to help you with your financial journey or to help you unpack issues in your past, make sure you make the investment in yourself.

Don't be too strong or too stingy with your money to invest in your financial and emotional self-care if you know that you need it.

So for **today's lifework,** I want you to read two articles.

I wrote "When Jesus Can't Fix It: How to Win With Therapy" to help women like us find affordable and quality mental health services.

Find it in Appendix E.

Similarly, I wrote "Should You Go Into Debt for an Out-of-Network Therapist?" to explain why I decided to pay more than I had to for therapy and why I didn't regret it.

It's located in Appendix F.

Each article asks you to take action. Write your thoughts and next steps for finding someone that you can talk to.

Who will you ask for help? For Day 41, tell us in The Happy Finances Community!

DAY 42

Maintain a Financial Gratitude Journal

If you've picked up *The Happy Finances Challenge*, then I know that you are ripe and ready for financial change in your life. What it also means is that you are ripe and ready for disappointment if you don't treat yourself lovingly and compassionately as you make major shifts in how you see yourself, how you see your money, and how you relate to both.

In short, there's a high probability that you will encounter financial setbacks during this journey and you will beat yourself up for not being perfect.

No bueno.

That's why **today's lifework** is super important, especially as we come to the end of the challenge. As you go through your financial life, with its ups and downs, you will need to keep track of what's working so you can keep moving forward.

My friend posted something on Facebook that was so poignant that I had to share it with you.

> The saying goes, "You can't see the forest amidst the trees." Sometimes it's hard to tell if I'm making progress when I have work up to my nose and I'm struggling to breathe. But when I'm done I get to take a step back and look at things from a distance and I can't believe the foundation that is in place.

What would be the first entry in your financial gratitude journal? After you write it below, buy yourself a journal dedicated to finding the good in your current financial situation.

_____

_____

_____

_____

_____

_____

_____

_____

_____

_____

_____

_____

_____

_____

_____

_____

_____

_____

_____

_____

_____

_____

_____

_____

_____

Share what your first entry of financial gratitude would be with us in The Happy Finances Community for Day 42.

DAY 43

Final Glow and Grow Report

Unlike the other weekly Growth Reports, I want you to reflect on your whole financial journey.

- Who are you now after 43 days of financial focus and work?
- Who do you see yourself becoming?

Be brutally honest. Use the space below to jot down your thoughts (prose, poetry), draw pictures, and memorable moments throughout this journey.

And if you're extra transformed, make a short video testimonial and share it with us in The Happy Finances Community.

We've been here in the trenches with you. We've been here rooting for you and we love to see the fruits of your hard work. ☺

_____
_____
_____
_____
_____
_____
_____
_____
_____
_____
_____
_____

A FINAL HAPPY NOTE

It's been really gratifying and fulfilling to write this book for you. As I wrote it, I relived some of the highest and lowest points of my financial journey.

And I know the woman that I was at the beginning of my journey is quite different than the woman that I am now.

What I am hoping is that picking up this book has made you feel inspired, energized, and committed to living a life full of personal growth and financial abundance.

I'm also hoping that it has given you the courage to continue on your journey—no matter how long or rough it will be.

I am always here to be a cheerleader and share in your success. Please hit me up and let me know how happy you are and how happy your finances are after completing The Happy Finances Challenge.

I'm all over these internet streets:

Twitter: @frugalfeminista
Instagram: @frugalfeminista
Pinterest: @frugalfeminista
Facebook: @TheFrugalFeminista

But you can always email me at kara@thefrugalfeminista.com.

Wishing you personal growth and financial liberation,

APPENDIX

APPENDIX A

MY FINANCIAL FAMILY TREE

Directions: Use this family tree to help you get to the root of your current financial thinking. Write down two or three of the biggest money messages you closest relatives.

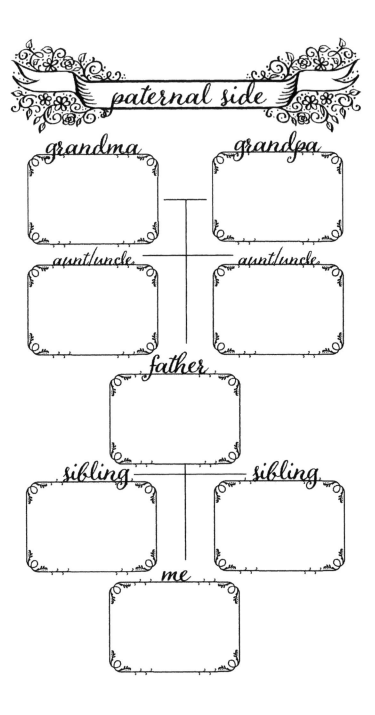

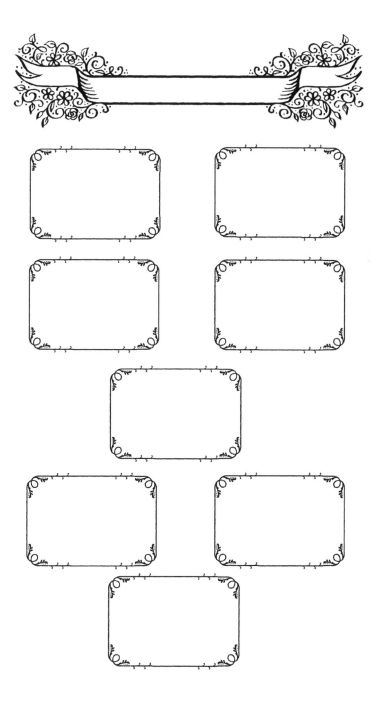

APPENDIX B

MONTHLY MAINTENANCE NUMBER WORKSHEET

Directions: It's time to find out how much it really costs to live your life. Take the following steps.

Step 1: Find your pay stubs, side hustle invoices, or any other income you collect every month. Calculate your total take-home pay.

Step 2: Write down ALL of your needs (i.e. food, rent) in the "needs" column, their amounts, and the total of ALL of your needs.

Step 3: Write down ALL of your wants (i.e. entertainment, clothes) in the "wants" column, their amounts, and the total of ALL of your wants.

Step 4: Add your "need" total and "wants" total. This is your Monthly Maintenance Number.

Needs		Wants	
Name of Expense	Amount	Name of Expense	Amount

Total:		**Total:**	

Total Monthly Maintenance Number (MMN): _____

Take-Home Pay: _____

Questions to Consider:

Is your MMN > your take-home pay?

  Answer: Reduce expenses and/or increase income.

Is your MMN < your take-home pay?

  Bravo! Keep going!

Is your MMN = your take-home pay?

  Answer: Reduce expenses and/or increase income. Why? You have NO wiggle room for money emergencies.

APPENDIX C

100 EASY SIDE HUSTLES

Sell Your Stuff: There are a lot of places online and offline where you can sell your unwanted things

1. Ebay
2. Etsy: Any handmade items can be sold here
3. Thredup: Will pay you for your gently-used clothes and shoes
4. Sell on Amazon: Sell merchandise or do dropshipping
5. Amazon Trade-In: Trade in your old electronics for cash
6. Have a yard sale
7. Consignment stores

Get Certified: These are cheap and easy certifications available online that can help bring in that extra cash

8. Notary public
9. Officiate Weddings

Rent Out Your Space

10. AirBnB
11. Liquidspace.com
12. Storewithme.com

Rent Out Your Stuff

13. Loanables.com
14. PeerRenters.com
15. Zilok.com

Use Your Car

16. Uber
17. Lyft
18. Turo: Rent out your car
19. Hyrecar.com: Rent out your car

20. Carvertise.com: Companies will pay you to put advertising on your car
21. Wrapify.com: Companies will pay you to put advertising on your car
22. Relay Rides: Car sharing

Be A Local Tour Guide: Many people will pay to have a local tour guide give them a personal tour

23. Toursbylocals.com
24. Showaround.com

Take Surveys

25. Swagbucks
26. InboxDollars
27. National Consumer Panel
28. Survey Junkie
29. Harris Poll
30. Opinion Outpost
31. Pinecone Research
32. Valued Opinion
33. MyPoints
34. VIP Voice
35. Ipsos Panel

Mystery Shopping: Be sure to avoid mystery shopping scams by going through a legit company like the ones listed below. MSPA http://www.mspa-na.org/ has a comprehensive list of all legitimate mystery shopping companies.

36. Marketforce
37. BestMark
38. Impact Marketing
39. Customer Perspectives

Small Tasks Or Errands

40. Task Rabbit
41. Gigwalk
42. MTurk microtasks
43. Clickworker.com

44. Postmates.com: Be paid to deliver packages to people
45. Zaarly.com
46. Yard Work
47. Cleaning
48. Closet organizing

Caregiving: You can find plenty of ways to housesit, pet sit, or babysit.

49. Rover.com: Pet sitting
50. MindmyHouse.com
51. Dog walking
52. Care.com
53. Sitter.com
54. Housesitter.com

Be Bart Of A Focus Or Test Group: Research and medical companies are always looking for people to join their focus groups.

55. CenterWatch.com
56. CISCRP.org
57. ClinicalTrials.gov
58. TestwiththeBest.com
59. PhRMA.org

Transcription

60. TranscribeMe
61. Quitate
62. Rev

Reviews

63. UserTesting: Review and test websites
64. Slicethepie.com: Review music

Use Your Skills: These are great ways to use skills that you already have.

65. Ghostwriting
66. Proofreading

67. Tutoring
68. Create resumes
69. Create an online course: Udemy
70. Bookkeeping
71. Sewing: seamstress and alterations
72. Be a local photographer
73. Shutterstock: Sell your stock photos
74. Voice123.com: Voiceover
75. Learn4good.com: Teach English
76. Event coordinator
77. Wedding Planner
78. Translate: If you're bilingual
79. Away 2 Be: Plan vacations
80. Baking
81. Catering
82. Moderate online forums
83. Fancy Hands: Virtual assistant
84. Computer coding: You can learn at codeacdemy.com
85. Zazzle.com: Design t-shirts
86. Skillshare.com
87. Threadless.com
88. Teespring.com
89. Programming
90. Website Design
91. Internet research
92. 99Designs: Graphic design
93. Savvyspreadsheets.com: Create and sell spreadsheet templates

Odd Things You Can Do And Sell

94. eJury.com
95. Sell plasma
96. Sell sperm
97. Buyandsellhair.com: Sell your hair
98. Rent-a-Friend.com
99. Become a professional cuddler
100. Become a professional line sitter

APPENDIX D

CREDIT CARD DEBT STATS WORKSHEET

Write down every credit and store card you own, the current balance, and the interest rates on each card. Add everything in the "Outstanding Balance" column to calculate your total debt.

Name of Credit Card/Store Card	Outstanding Balance	Interest Rates

Total Debt: _____

APPENDIX E

WHEN JESUS CAN'T FIX IT:
HOW TO WIN WITH THERAPY

Therapy saved my life. Seriously. There was a time in my life where I was eating, sleeping, and living in a very, very dark hopeless place. And I knew that the only way that I was going to pull myself out of this depression was with the guided, consistent help of a professional that I felt comfortable and safe around.

For those of you that read what I just wrote, saw themselves in my testimony, and are ready to find a "right fit" therapist, here are some of the steps to take to ensure that your journey to selecting one is as smooth as possible.

Think about who you want your therapist to be. Since you will be exploring some of the most personal and intimate parts of your life, you will have to be comfortable and trust your therapist. You will have to get clear about who you trust the most. Would you prefer a male or female? Would you prefer a therapist of a particular age, religious background, country of origin, race, and age?

I know for me, I need the support of a woman of color who would not use any religious perspective when providing support or coping strategies. I also knew that I wanted a person around my age so my sessions would seem more casual and less clinical.

Start the process before you are in crisis. It's important to know that therapists are often in session and will not answer texts, emails, or phone calls in real time. On top of that, they often work alone— meaning that they are their own secretary, which may delay their response times. And finally, with reputable therapists, you may encounter that they are booked for weeks, if not months, when you need to see them. So be vigilant about monitoring your emotions.

When you get early signs that you are in need of help, don't dawdle on getting it. It may take more than you think.

Be prepared to go on some "therapist dates." Therapist dates is a term that I use to describe the process that I underwent to find the ideal therapist for me. Like romantic dating, you have to kiss a few frogs before you find your princess or prince.

Before finding my current therapist, I reached out to at least 15 different therapists for phone consultations. Shortly after speaking to a range of therapists, I created a short list of viable therapists based on how I felt about our sessions. I booked at least one session with each of those short-list therapists. After a few sessions, it became easy to identify the therapist that I wanted to continue working with.

In each of the sessions, I had the chance to assess the type of questions they asked, the observations they made about my life circumstances, the level of attention they gave to me, and other nuanced factors that could only be unearthed when you are working with a therapist.

Speak with your insurance representative. Therapy can be quite costly. If you have insurance, please reach out to your carrier for recommendations. If you are able to connect with an in-network therapist, you can save a lot of money. If, on the other hand, you find an out-of-network, your insurance provider will give you all the information that you need about deductibles, the amount of time it takes to process claims, and the types of forms you will need to fill out to ensure timely reimbursements, if applicable.

It's unfortunate that our society doesn't see attending to emotional and mental disease like anxiety, loneliness, and depression with the same sense of urgency that we seem to place on attending to a failing kidney, diabetes, or a broken leg.

So if you feel that you require ER-level emotional support, then you are going to have to make it your priority to get it.

APPENDIX F

SHOULD YOU GO INTO DEBT FOR AN OUT-OF-NETWORK THERAPIST?

It was September 2015. I was three months pregnant and having *all day* sickness. The sight of my husband made me mad and his smell drove me crazy. To make matters worse, I was also three months into a new position at work.

The toxic work culture was taking its toll; I switched to survival mode. I fully stopped getting my hair done or ironing my clothes, but I pushed myself to bathe, even though that was a battle.

I cried all the time: in the shower, in the car, and on my way home.

Despite all of these stresses, I continued to beat-up on myself, "Stop crying, Kara. What do you have to cry about? Just woman-up and push through."

But the bottom was clearly dropping out.

Denial allowed me to function a little longer. That was until I found myself spending my Christmas vacation alone on my couch desperately searching *Psychology Today* for emergency counseling.

My Out-of-Network Experience

My first day of therapy started in mid-January 2016 with Toni. She was young, kind, and gave me the right amount of push and support. She was also out-of-network, which meant she was expensive; my insurance would only partially foot the bill for my sessions because, technically, I could have received similar services from the many in-network counselors and therapists.

And God knows I tried to go the cost-effective, in-network route.

But it wasn't adding up.

Very few of the therapists I reached out to returned my call for an initial appointment; and for those that did, I didn't feel a connection. There was no chemistry. I didn't feel that I could trust, confide in, or feel vulnerable with them, in which case-making progress is virtually impossible.

How Much Does Therapy Cost?

When I finally made the decision to work with Toni, I had to call my health insurance provider to crunch the numbers. Each 60-minute session cost $150. I had a $150 deductible and insurance was willing to pay $55 for each of my sessions. So, I had to pay $95 out-of-pocket each session, which amounted to $380 a month.

I religiously attended therapy for 11 months. So, in total, I paid $4,180. Without insurance, I would have had to pay $7,200. If I had chosen one of the therapists from my network, which had a co-pay of $15, I would have only had to pay $660.

Cost of Therapy At-a-Glance

Therapy without insurance: $7,200
Therapy with insurance (out-of-network): $4,180
Therapy with insurance (in-network): $660

How Much Is Too Much?

Based on these numbers, I could have saved big time on therapy had I settled for therapists in my network. But that's just it—I would have settled. From the time that I emailed Toni to inquire about her services to the little nudges she would give me to come in when I was feeling discouraged and the continued support she provides even though I no longer see her—I would have to say the only thing that I lost in this situation was money.

It sounds obnoxious to write that as many of us struggle with a range of competing expenses. But when I made a commitment to investing in my emotional health and happiness, I literally had to put my money where my mouth was.

I liken the process of looking for a therapist to that of looking for a partner. While it would have been nice if my husband were independently wealthy, it wasn't necessary for love. Similarly, I would have been ecstatic to find an in-network therapist that I loved.

But I didn't.

The experience of finding a therapist helped me really understand the difference between cost and worth. Cost is the dollar amount that we place on a good or bad service. Worth is a little deeper and extremely personal. Since I valued my emotional health and realized that I needed support in reestablishing my self-respect and identity, I knew that choosing the more expensive option would make the most sense for me and my goals.

How Therapy Eventually Paid for Itself

In therapy, I had the chance to rebuild myself and rewrite the narrative I told myself and others about who I was. Through my inner work I cultivated the courage to establish and maintain boundaries. I also gained a deep level of respect for my feelings, an awareness of my passions, and deep trust in my ability to make the best decisions for my life and my newborn baby.

In concrete terms, between the time that I started and ended therapy, I left that toxic position, found a new one where I was valued for my contributions, nearly doubled my revenue and client base for The Frugal Feminista, and felt better in my skin.

So should you go a little broke for mental health? My answer: yes.

Made in the USA
Columbia, SC
13 June 2020